To all who yearn for freedom.
In memory of my great-grandfather
Isaac Copper, USCT, a cofounder
of Unionville, Maryland
—Carole Boston Weatherford

For Michael Svensson
—R. Gregory Christie

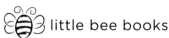 little bee books

An imprint of Bonnier Publishing Group
853 Broadway, New York, New York 10003
Text copyright © 2016 by Carole Boston Weatherford
Illustrations copyright © 2016 by R. Gregory Christie
LITTLE BEE BOOKS is a trademark of Bonnier Publishing Group, and
associated colophon is a trademark of Bonnier Publishing Group.
Manufactured in China LEO 0815
First Edition 10 9 8 7 6 5 4 3 2 1
Library of Congress Cataloging-in-Publication Data is available upon request.
ISBN 978-1-4998-0103-3
littlebeebooks.com
bonnierpublishing.com

FREEDOM IN CONGO SQUARE

by
Carole Boston Weatherford

illustrated by
R. Gregory Christie

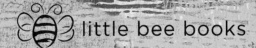
little bee books

Foreword
by Freddi Williams Evans

Congo Square is an open space located within Louis Armstrong Park in New Orleans, Louisiana. Many events have taken place there during New Orleans' history, including ball games, circus performances, fireworks shows, and police drills. But it was the music, songs, and dances performed by enslaved Africans on Sunday afternoons that made Congo Square known worldwide. These Africans had been captured in West and Central West Africa, separated from their families, placed in chains aboard slave ships, and brought to the new land as property. Some were also brought from the West Indies and other parts of the United States.

In New Orleans, they worked Mondays through Saturdays from sunup to sundown, clearing swamps, cutting roads, building houses, growing crops, washing, cooking, cleaning, and whatever else they were told. But based on a law called the Code Noir, Sundays were holy days. They were to be work-free and set aside for worship. In addition to attending church, some enslaved people used that time off to earn money by growing and selling food, hunting, fishing, or working for their owners and other people.

On Sunday afternoons, people of African heritage, both enslaved and free, came together to enjoy themselves. They met at different places in the city until a law made Congo Square the only place they could meet. There, they formed circles around groups of dancers and musicians in different parts of the square. Inside those circles, musicians played instruments like the ones they knew in their homelands, including different kinds and sizes of drums along with string and wind instruments. The dances originated in parts of West and Central West Africa and included the Calinda,

Bamboula, Juba, and the Congo. Those who stood around joined in by clapping, singing, and shaking gourd rattles.

At Congo Square, enslaved people who had lived in other states as well as other parts of Louisiana introduced different styles of songs, dances, and instruments, including European styles. Over time the intermingling of the different African, Caribbean, and European styles led to the development of new styles, including jazz music, which is now performed around the world. The music for jazz funerals and for second-line dancing and parades, along with the music of Mardi Gras Indians, all began in New Orleans and are all based on the style called jazz.

Congo Square was placed on the National Register of Historic Places in 1993, and a historical marker was erected there in 1997. Although "Congo Square" has been its unofficial name since the mid-1800s, it has held many other names including Place Publique, Circus Square, Congo Plains, and Beauregard Square. In 2011 the New Orleans City Council passed an ordinance that made Congo Square the official name of this national landmark.

Today, thanks to the Congo Square Preservation Society, New Orleanians of all ages and backgrounds, along with visitors from all parts of world, come together in Congo Square on Sundays. There, they enjoy the freedom of expressing themselves by singing, dancing, drumming, and playing other musical instruments of their choice. If you are ever in New Orleans on a Sunday afternoon, feel free to join in.

Freddi Williams Evans is a historian and Congo Square expert. Find out more about her at freddievans.com.

Mondays, there were hogs to slop,
mules to train, and logs to chop.

Slavery was no ways fair.
Six more days to Congo Square.

Tuesdays, there were cows to feed,
fields to plow, and rows to seed.

A moment without work was rare.
Five more days to Congo Square.

Wednesdays, there were beds to make,
silver to shine, and bread to bake.

The dreaded lash, too much to bear.
Four more days to Congo Square.

Thursdays, there were clothes to clean,
floors to scrub, and babes to wean.

Spirituals rose from the despair.
Three more days to Congo Square.

Fridays, there were crops to pick,
trees to prune, and walls to brick.

Run away, run away. Some slaves dared.
Two more days to Congo Square.

Saturdays, there were beans to can,
hens to pluck, and folks to fan.

Freedom was slaves' ardent prayer.
One more day to Congo Square.

Week in, week out, from sun to sun,
always more chores to be done.

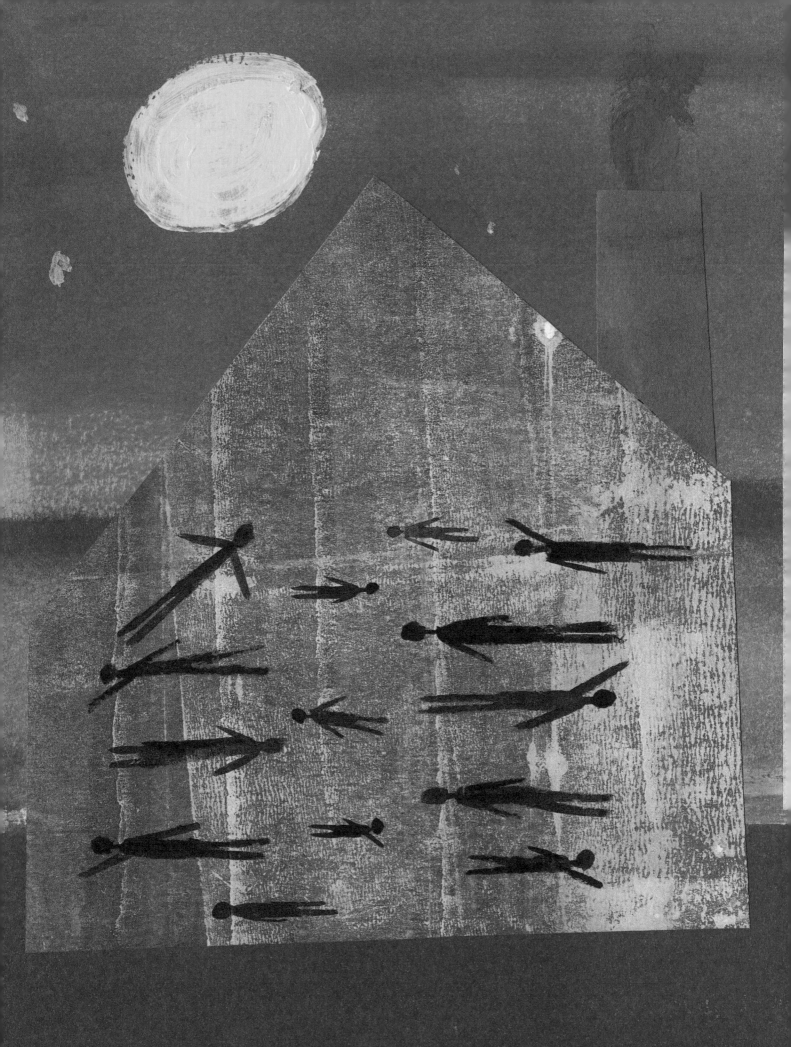

And even as the plantation slept,
wood was on the fire kept.

But Sunday was a day of rest,
when Master charmed the weekend guests.

Slaves had off one afternoon,
when the law allowed them to commune.

They flocked to New Orleans' Congo Square.
Sundays, slaves and free met there.

It was a market and a gathering ground
where African music could resound.

Beneath the sun in the open air,
the crowd abuzz with news to share.

Grouped by nation, language, tribe,

they drummed ancestral roots alive.

They played triangles, gourds, and bells,

banzas, flutes, fiddles, and shells.

Women in gauze, silk, and percale,

men in fringe and furry tails

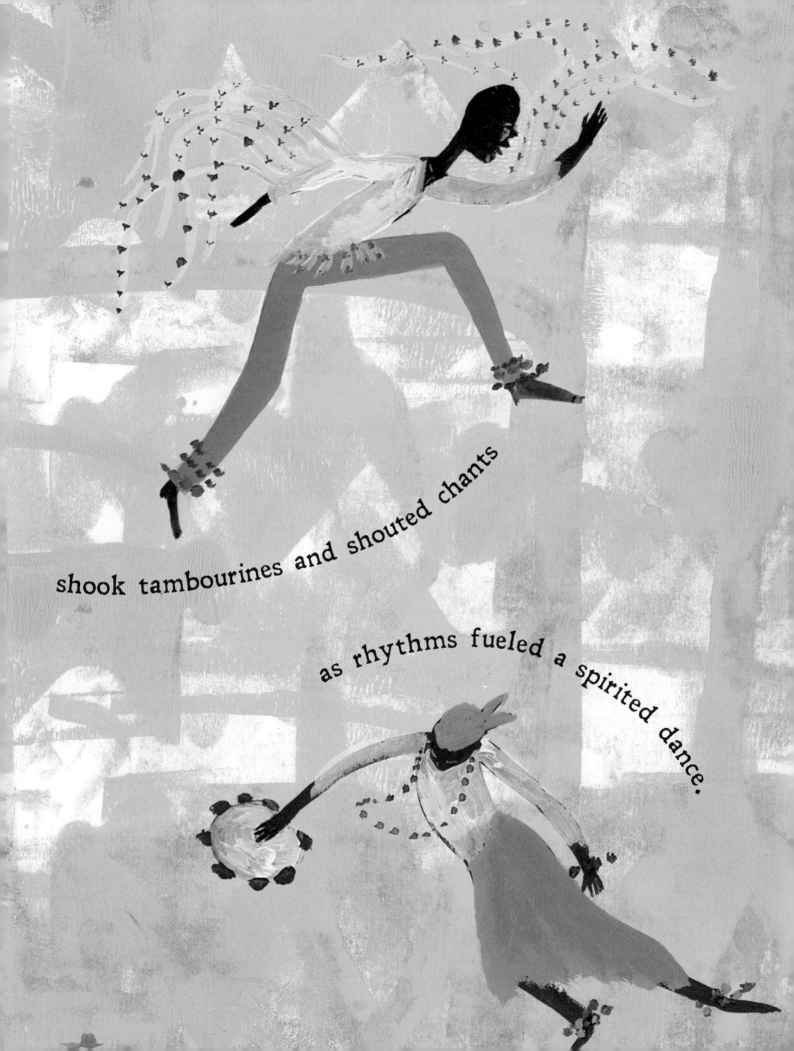

shook tambourines and shouted chants

as rhythms fueled a spirited dance.

They rejoiced as if they had no cares;
half day, half free in Congo Square.

This piece of earth was a world apart.
Congo Square was freedom's heart.

Glossary

Ardent \'är-dənt\: showing or having warmth of feeling; passionate

Banza \'B£n-zə\: gourd instrument that originates from Africa; the ancestor of the modern banjo

Commune \kə-'myün\: to share one's intimate thoughts or feelings with someone or something

Gauze \'gȯz\: a thin translucent fabric of silk, linen, or cotton

Gourd \'gȯrd\: any of a family of tendril-bearing vines (such as the cucumber, melon, squash, and pumpkin)

Percale \(ˌ)pər-'kāl\: a closely woven fine cotton or polyester fabric

Prune \'prün\: to cut off the parts of a woody plant that are dead or not wanted

Resound \ri-'zaȯnd\: to fill a place with sound; be loud enough to echo

Slop \'släp\: waste food used to feed pigs or other animals

Spiritual \'spir-i-chə-wəl\: a religious folk song of a deeply emotional character

Wean \'wēn\: to accustom an infant to food other than his or her mother's milk

Author's Note

Before becoming part of the United States, Louisiana was first a French colony and then a Spanish colony. At the time, a law set aside Sundays as a day of rest. In Louisiana, even slaves had Sundays off from work. That observance continued after the Louisiana Purchase when the territory became part of the United States.

On their free day, slaves in New Orleans were allowed to gather at various locations in the city. In 1817, however, a city law designated one location for slaves' Sunday gatherings. The mayor chose an open field just outside the city on the edge of the Treme Plantation. The meeting place went by various names—Place des Negres, Place Publique, Beauregard Square, Circus Square, Place Congo, and others—before becoming known as Congo Square.

Each week, hundreds of slaves and free blacks flocked to Congo Square. In most states, slaves were not allowed to assemble without white supervision, and African music was banned. Elsewhere in the New World, slaves were forbidden to own African drums. But in Congo Square, African rhythms, culture, and customs had free expression and were preserved. Descendants of Africa could speak African languages, practice African religious beliefs, do African dances, and play and sing African music. The musicians played not only violins, but also instruments with roots in Africa: drums, gourds, marimbas, tambourines, and the banza, which is a banjo-like instrument. Local whites and out-of-town visitors came to the square to experience the lively music and dance.

But there was more to these gatherings than revelry. For black residents of New Orleans, Congo Square was a hub of communication. Slaves and free blacks shared news and concerns from their respective communities. Sometimes, they socialized in tribal groupings. The square was also a marketplace. Vendors—enslaved and free—sold produce they had grown, herbs they had gathered, wild game they had hunted, or goods they had made by hand. For a few hours every Sunday, Congo Square gave slaves a taste of freedom.

After slavery was abolished in 1865, music remained a vital part of Congo Square. In the late nineteenth century, the square was host to brass band concerts by Creole musicians. Congo Square is now part of Louis Armstrong Park, which is named after the jazz great and New Orleans native. That is fitting since jazz, America's only original art form, evolved from the African rhythms kept alive in Congo Square. Today, Congo Square is listed on the National Register of Historic Places, and New Orleans is known as the birthplace of jazz.

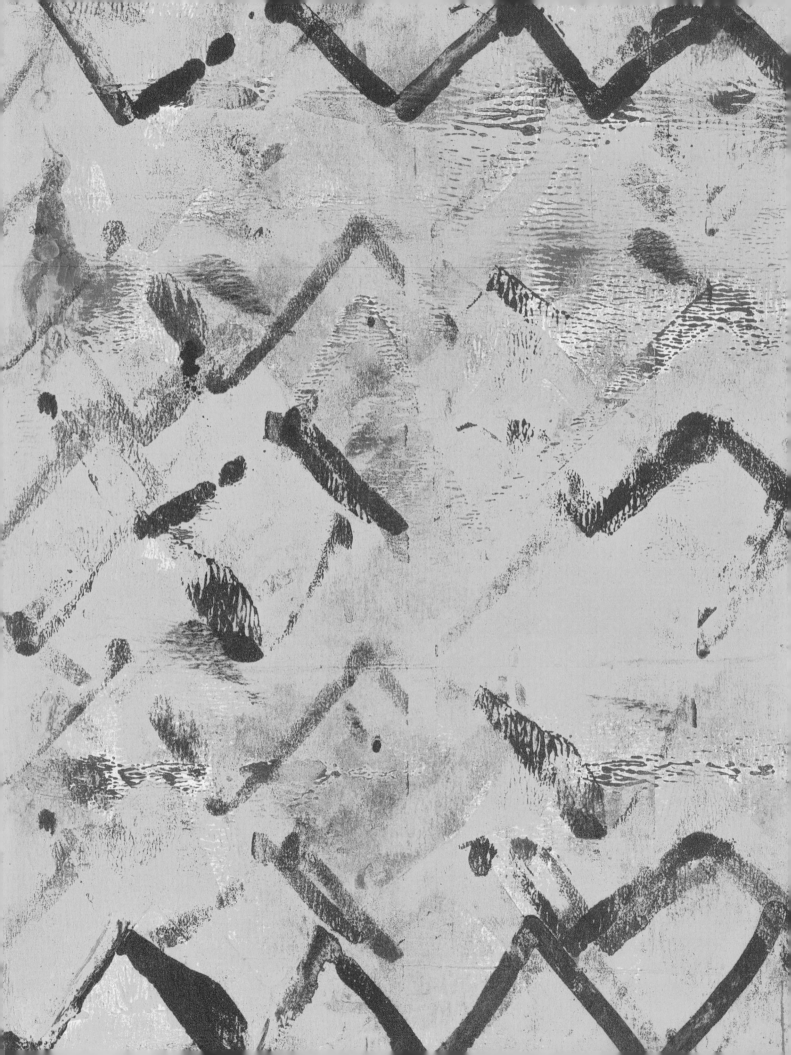